**THE TRUE MEANING BEHIND THE TITLE**

Sandra Calvert CA CPA
John Petty FCA FCPA

Copyright © 2018 by Sandra Calvert and John Petty.

Cover design and illustrations by Sandra Calvert and Richard Foster.

Design and typesetting by Richard Foster.

Production and Database right by Sandra Calvert [maker].

The rights of Sandra Calvert and John Petty to be identified as the Author of all Work has been asserted by them in accordance with the Copyright, Designs and Patents Act 1988 and Copyright Act 1968 (Cth).

All rights reserved. No part of this publication may be reproduced, stored in a retrieval system or transmitted in any form or by any means, electronic, mechanical, photocopying, scanning, recording or otherwise, without the prior written permission and consent of the publisher, or as expressly permitted by law, or under terms agreed with the appropriate reprographic rights organisation. Enquiries concerning reproduction outside the scope of the above should be sent to the reproduction request department at email sales@coachability.net.au .

You must not circulate this book in any other binding or cover and you must impose this same condition on any acquirer.

The publisher has used its best endeavours to ensure that any persons, businesses, articles or associations referred to in this book are correct at the time of going to press. However, the publisher and authors have no responsibility for other parties as to their accuracy or completeness. The publisher and author have used their best efforts in preparing this book, they make no representations or warranties with respect to the accuracy or completeness of the contents of this book and specifically disclaim any implied warranties of merchantability or fitness for a particular person. No warranty may be created or extended by sales representatives or written sales materials. The advice, strategies and guidance may not be suitable for your situation. You should always consult with a professional where appropriate. The publisher has made every effort to mark as such all words which it believes to be trademarks. The publisher should also like to make it clear that the presence of a word in the book, whether marked or unmarked, in no way affects its legal status as a trademark. Neither the publisher nor author shall be liable for any loss of profit or any other commercial damages, including but not limited to special, incidental, consequential, or other damages.

Published by Sanvon Investments Pty Ltd.

Australian Library Cataloguing in Publication Date: a catalogue record for this title is available from the Australian Library.

 eISBN 978-0-6450607-8-2

 ISBN 978-0-646-99576-2.

*Dedicated to creating
awareness of the valuable strategic
business partnership role
that the CFO provides.*

Contents

Abstract	1
Introduction	2
EVOLUTION of the CFO	3
DEFINE the CFO	6
ROLES of the CFO	8
CFO Reporting Framework	9
CHARACTER OF the CFO	10
CFO as the M&M of PERFORMANCE	12
RESEARCH of the CFO	12
The Future CFO	14
Conclusion	15
Acknowledgements	16
Reference List	16

Abstract

The role of a CFO and value that a CFO provides has seen a number of disparate definitions of the role. In this article, we analyse the evolution of the position through time and its progression into the future. We are interested in unravelling the differing evaluations of the CFO through our findings to create clarity to the workforce and educational sector. We consider how the role interfaces within the hierarchal chain and to the added value provided to those in governance. We demonstrate how the CFO adds value and in so doing, is a dynamic pivotal executive in an organisation. We conclude with a greater appreciation and understanding of who the current CFO is and the future of such.

Introduction

What do you think when you read the title CFO? Some say Chief Financial Officer and others say CFO. Have you wondered how recruiters, CEO's and Boards employ a CFO with such confusion from the onset with the title? How do they engage the right person and to what role does the CFO perform? We discuss the CFO title at length of how it is to be displayed and the connotation behind the title to grasp a greater understanding to assist in the heirearchal appreciation of this co-partner or co-pilot to the CEO. We provide clarity of the role the CFO is to perform and skill sets required for the role, as we step through the evolution of the CFO to the current and future importance of this role that has entrenched this confusion and seen the majority of CFO's under-utilised.

To answer these questions we will encapture and unravel the insight of a CFO from three main sources. Firstly from those we found to have promulgated on the subject. Secondly from those who have practiced as a CFO and finally from those who have mentored and taught CFO's since inception. Our research enabled us to share the character of a CFO to inturn develop the CFO reporting framework, that aids in the CFO as the strategic partner.

Harnessing the insight from the founder of the CFO training workshop since 1995, we ask Mr John Petty, for his erudition and observations, enabling a collation of the best measures of a CFO in utilising the best of the newest tools and emerging discussions.

EVOLUTION OF THE CFO

Akin to stories of how mankind evolved, so to has that of the CFO. The most common discussion was that the CFO was the most senior accountant. This is a fair assumption, but understanding the CFO requires us to step through evolution from the accountant to the CFO.

The historical recognition from ancient records, suggest that accounting as a role began with bartering in the stone age. Barter is the ability to value goods and services to provide a basis with which to trade. The trade highlighted the need to accurately account for the value of goods and services traded in consideration of the costs, accounted for by a bookkeeper and abacus. As barter transitioned into monetary trade with increasing compliance of taxation, there was a need and hence subsequent recognition for those who could perform beyond the use of an abacus or ledger, to consolidate and interpret information from a mathematical format to a meaningful analysis of historical data. A new role was born, one that saw a quantitative expert as a necessity for business, it was, The Accountant.

The Association of CPA (Certified Practicing Accountant) set the recognition in 1896 founding the first association of accountants. It was from the generic title of Senior Accountant that the foundation was laid for Accountants to be recognised as the reporting hub of financial information within an organisation. As Hatfield, Sanders and Burton (1940, p.3) expanded upon this in Accounting- Principles and Practices, `Accounting is a science, in the sense that it provides a systematic treatment and classification for the transactions and conditions which must be recorded'[1]. It was this recognition of analytics that would become paramount in the future to the evolution of accounting. The importance Accountants played in organisations as historical data compilation and interpretation experts to achieve budgets, reined in the recognition and respect of accountants where titles arose.

Financial Controller was a title of longevity describing the most senior expert within the organisation to control the finances and scorekeepers of the finances, until the 1990's when the Finance Manager emerged. Recognition of a qualified Accountant holding a post graduate Chartered Accountant or Certified Practicing Accountant degree with a role requiring leadership qualities to manage, was a key turning point in what would have remained an otherwise quantitative role. This point is pivotal in the reshaping of an industry that was heading fast toward technical advancements that would see an enormous revaluation of incumbents in an organisation.

The Finance Manager is the informant of all financial information in analytical format and historical format, providing essential insight as to the performance of the organisation transacted through accounting software. The measures used saw steps taken to report on external measures such as benchmarking against other quantitative data, yet restricted to financial acumen. So why is there a CFO? Is there a demand for a CFO or was this a retitle of the Finance Manager?

Chief Financial Officer was a correct understanding when the title first came about. The role was that of a Finance Manager (FM), however it did not provide a differentiation to the FM, nor become the much needed Second in Charge (2IC) for the CEO. Confusion of how to become the business partner to the CEO and strategic organisational partner was overcome with a remarkable breakthrough. The BSC Balanced Scorecard took financial and non-financial reporting to the next step, to measure in alignment to organisational strategy. The link of alignment was the largest step forward in a rapidly transforming era of global interaction and technical advancements. Boards began to place more pressure on rapid transformative response times and visions that the CEO would create to encompass active growth within a shorter time frame.

The CEO was looking at the organisation internally, rather than externally focussing on the challenges and opportunities ahead, leaving minimal time to create the vision in this repetitive stressful circle. This void would be the final underpinning of a new role emergence, one that moulded the key executive who could lead and perform the strategic role as Co-Pilot to the CEO, that would be the Chief Financial Officer. However leaving the word Financial in the title was not conducive to the many roles undertaken by this executive. Hence the word Financial was dropped to be replaced by a singular letter 'F' , representing a distinction as a key executive with accounting qualities performing a majority of non-financial duties, thus establishing CFO.

It is for this reason that the CFO is sometimes known as a CPO in many countries, the Chief Performance Officer, being the value creator, measurer and creator of performance. It would be easier to recognise a title of CPO that represented the requests for information interpretation and strategic suggestions toward key business drivers and qualitative and quantitative data. Inside HR magazine, (`What's behind the rise of the chief performance officer?' 2016) describe the CPO role and how it has emerged from being a CFO, `The chief performance officer is a new and influential position emerging among C-suite ranks, in response to increased demands from boards and greater levels of complexity and sophistication in business[2].'

InsideHR continue their findings to determine their studies were of the view that a CFO was a Finance role. This analogy conflicts with that practised since 1995 by John Petty as a key note speaker for CA and CPA educating future CFO's that finance is a minor role. Petty does foster holding a post graduate degree as a CA, CPA or with a GAA affiliated association as a pre-requisite to being able to interpret and request the information required both financially and non-financially with a 90% loading on qualitative information.

The corroborative claim to John Petty's overview is dictated in the same InsideHR article stating, `CFOs now have to focus much more on the key business drivers and information flows that help predict business performance quickly and consistently.[2]'

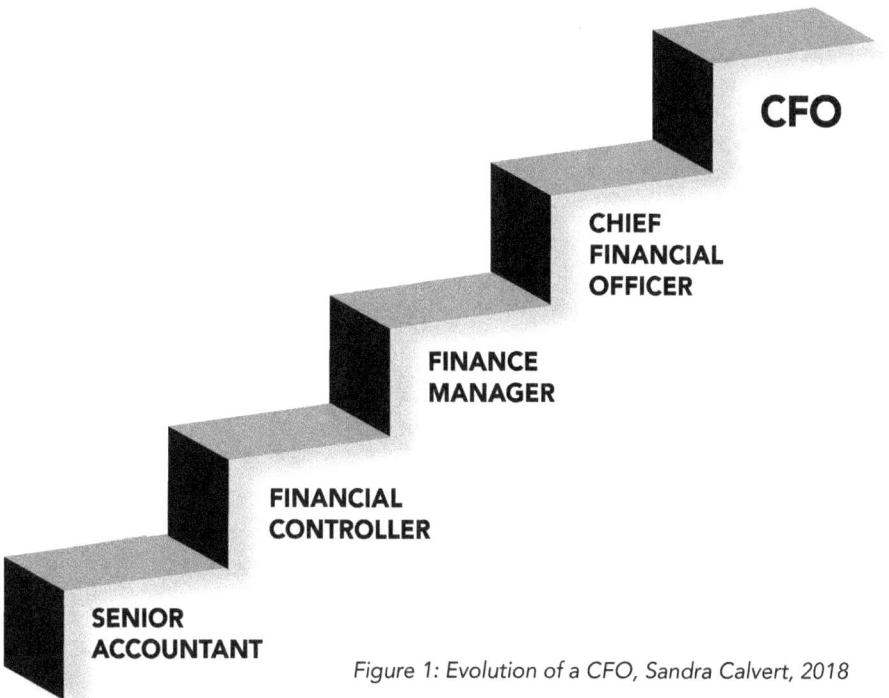

Figure 1: Evolution of a CFO, Sandra Calvert, 2018

DEFINE THE CFO

The CFO evolution has provided our research with the foundation to establish a concise definition of the term CFO. IBM have undertaken in-depth studies of the C-Suite to recognise that the CFO is the second in charge as figure 2 depicts in IBM's C-Suite hierarchy chart and reporting spectre[2]. The heirarchy does not devalue the roles played in the C-Suite, notwithstanding it does yield vital clarity as to the key source and hierarchical information channel from within the C-Suite. The information channel flows to the CFO to analyse, consolidate, extract and determine for reporting, though it is not the only information required, from within the C-Suite. This dynamic strategic role as the Elevator of Information as the IBM C-Suite heirarchy[2] demonstrates, requires a CFO to Monitor and Measure Performance of the organisation.

A CFO does not replace the CEO nor perform the duties of the CEO. The CEO is the pilot, steering the organisation toward successful achievement of the strategic goal, looking externally for opportunities, threats and challenges, whereas the CFO is the co-pilot looking in and leading the organisation strategically. A common slang word for this co-partner or second in charge is 2-I-C. The 2IC role for the CEO is now fulfilled by the CFO. The large responsibility to observe the entire operations of the organisation is given to the CFO. Our appreciation and respect as to why this has occurred can be easily explained.

The reason the CFO is selected above the remainder of the C-Suite is due to being a recognised central hub for information traffic, and possessing an educated skillset required to interpret, analyse and report on all aspects of financial and non-financial data.

IBM provided an insight in a further 2015 study focussing on CFO's to confirm this theory (IBM 2015, p.14) `make sure your organisation's financial planning is fully aligned with its strategic and operational planning' and to `evaluate the impact of emerging technologies on every aspect of your enterprise'[3].

Many characteristics are required by a CFO to align with the leadership of management and the board. Characteristics of the CFO are discussed later in this journal.

THE CUSTOMER-ACTIVATED ENTERPRISE
Insights from the Global C-suite Study.

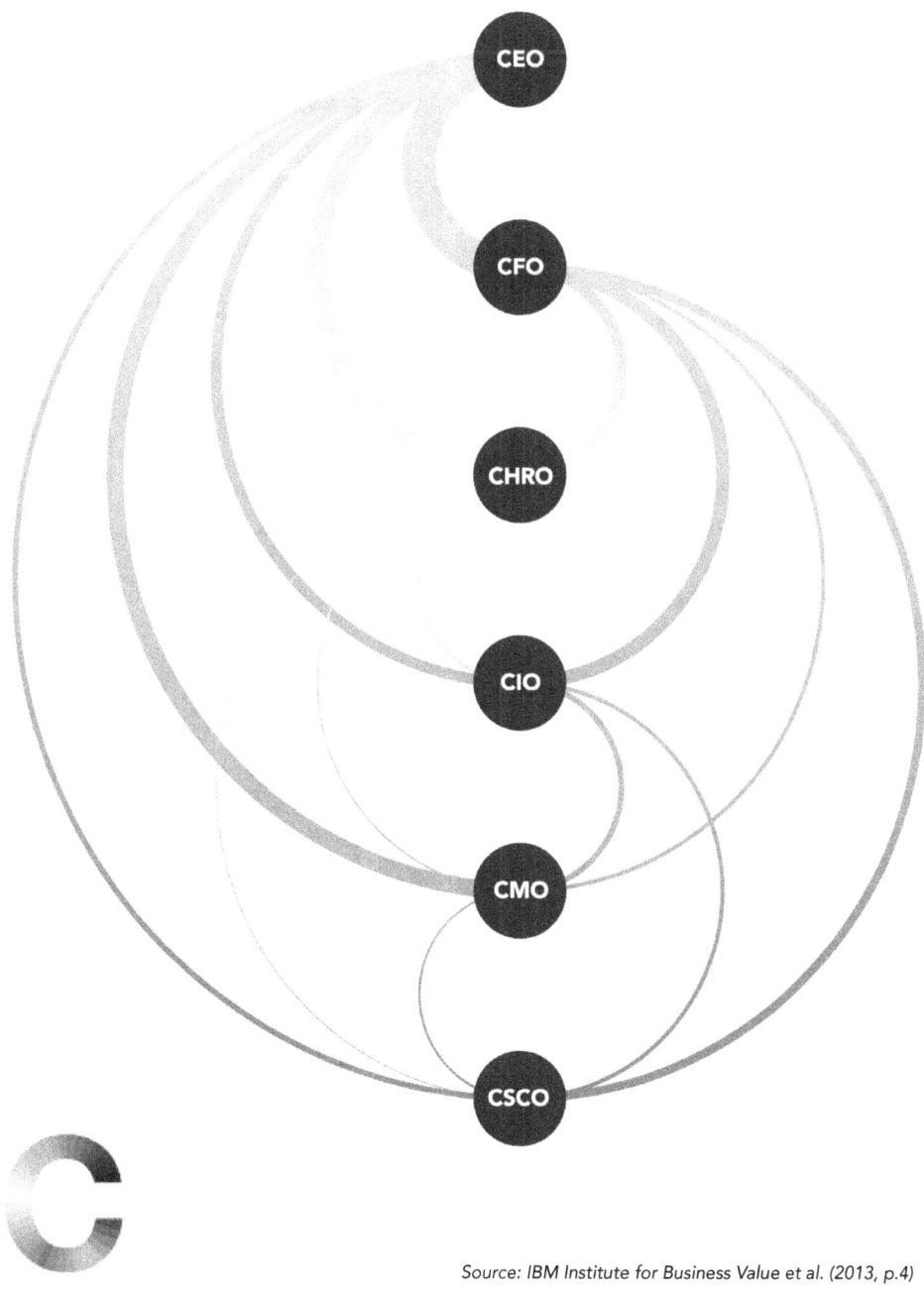

Source: IBM Institute for Business Value et al. (2013, p.4)

Figure 2: CxOs from an intricate web of relationships

ROLES OF THE CFO

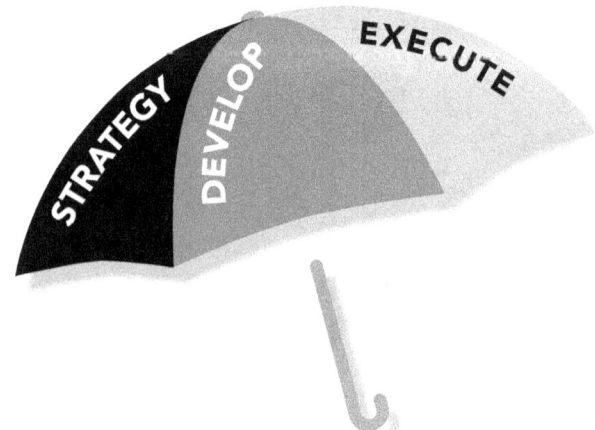

Figure 3: Roles of the CFO, Sandra Calvert, 2018

As a Co-Pilot to the CEO and the conductor of information, the CFO performs an important role to filter the raw information received, harnessing what is known to find the unknown using specific measuring tools. The result is meaningful measurable information reported to the appropriate channels in a tailored end user easy-to-interpret format. It is this process of input, deflection, attraction and output that can be hypothesised as holding the Umbrella of the Organisation acting as a conduit of information between the Shareholders, CEO, Board, C-Suite and Management that harnesses their skillset in one of the most important roles as the gatekeeper and information strategist. It is at this point where all information is gathered, measured as to what matters, assessed and reported that could also be regarded as the Funnel of information.

Performing numerous critical tasks, the CFO is the lead information analyst with the responsibility to ask the key questions of the C-Suite to align to the short term and long term Strategic Plan of the organisation. A solid understanding of the Strategic Plan cast by the Board, through the Vision of the CEO, will shape the reporting and subsequent analysis and involvement that the CFO requests of the C-Suite.

There are 3 elements required by the CFO role, refer to Figure 3. The first element is to identify key drivers and to create a Strategy that includes the transformative business model and plan. Having established the strategy the second element is to Develop channels through the use of measuring what matters, and managing the internal business processes and key information required to channel through the correct communications. The third and final step is to Execute the strategy and processes to create the growth. Execution of the strategic plan through solid controls, liaising with major parties including those within the organisation, to then implement to penetrate the market. To further understand the role, it is necessary to recognise the reporting framework.

CFO Reporting Framework

Frameworks are a key driver to successful reporting. The IBM CFO study comprised of 4,183 CxO's from more than 20 industries that included 576 CFOs worldwide in addition to their former research of 23,000 interviews. The CFO study provided the reporting order within the organisations that have a C-Suite with the exception of larger organisations that may have additional higher ranking leaders such as a Director of Finance. From the findings of the heirarchy and in addition to over 1,000 elite CFO's across Australia and New Zealand that we have professionally educated, we can constitute the reporting framework of a CFO.

To Ask – raise aberrative questions that matter of other C-Suite executives and/or Management, to alert, highlight, query and update on information required.

To Analyse – align the organisation's strategic goals and subsequent targets through analysis

To Report – provide two disparate powerful and meaningful reports; to the CEO to forward to the board providing strategical and minimal tactical information to assist the decision making ; and provide to Management information that is operational and tactical.

To Strategise – align the analytic outcomes to the strategic goals of the organisation, harnessing the unique tools of a CFO to design and lead the organisation.

No longer is the CFO role a majority finance function due to the change in nature of the role, rather the role is the flow of information from the C-Suite through the reporting framework that is designed, analysed and constructed by the CFO, as summarised in Table 1.

Talent Management	CHRO	Chief Human Resource Officer
Risk	CSO	Chief Security Officer
Operations	COO	Chief Operating Officer
Finance	CFO	CFO
Marketing	CMO	Chief Marketing Officer
Analyst	CBA	Chief Business Analyst
Administration	CAO	Chief Administrative Officer
Research & Development	CEO	Chief Executive Officer
Information Technology	CIO	Chief Intelligence Officer
Sustainability	CSO	Chief Sustainability Officer

Table 1: CFO Reporting Framework, Sandra Calvert, 2018

Table 1 highlights the reliance on the C-Suite to provide the CFO with the information the CFO requests, investigates and analyses, that is paramount to the information required for reporting, planning and strategic purposes.

CHARACTER OF the CFO

An ideal character of a CFO would encompass the following traits:

Leadership	Solution Provider
Strategic	High Control Management
Visionary	Talent Scout/Awareness
Analytic	Organised
Ethical	Intrapreneur
Technical Awareness	Self Driven
Risk Awareness	Focussed
External Market Awareness	Decisive
Financial Awareness	Communicative
Problem Solver	Empathetic

Other Compulsory attributes:
- 15+ years experience working in industry
- Be a full CA, CPA or other GAA member

It is important to recognise the character of candidates when employing a CFO or improving one's own skill sets to become a CFO. Reading a business book does not traditionally metamorphosis one into an organised or decisive CFO. The inner traits are the key drivers of aspiring and accomplished leaders. Business books are to assist in providing additional and unknown tools and knowledge for readers, that must be appreciated from a textbook smart perspective. It is the physical work experience that must be achieved as it will be required to draw on instantaneously as problems arise.

A CFO will often address shareholders at an AGM, where an array of different personal skill sets are required in order to communicate in a professional, confident, friendly, reassuring manner and be able to respond to and/or answer questions in an understanding and diplomatic manner. The very nature of communicating and respect to those when raising questions, will determine the extent of detail and honest answers that are shared by stakeholders to the CFO. The uniqueness of public speaking is often overlooked when selecting a CFO for a new role.

The internal organisation focus imperative to a CFO requires external awareness in order to monitor, measure, assess, compare and report, hence the character traits listed above to include awareness of various external potential disruptive factors to performance and growth. The internal organisation focus also requires a CFO to assess whether the staff are competent, capable or require upskilling or changing to suit new and improved technology introduced in-house and the rapidly changing market demands pushing products and services into evolving demands.

Conclusively the CFO will be a very strong leader, open to suggestions and resolve, yet able to fill the gap the CEO once had as their reliable informant of all issues that can be measured and that matter.

CFO as the M&M of PERFORMANCE

The term Monitor and Measure has been mentioned in this article however the term deserves greater emphasis as it forms a considerable skill foundation from which many tools are used by a CFO to report. Reporting by a CFO will be non financial and financial, both in the format of dashboards.

A CFO will Monitor changes to the organisation's performance both from external and internal factors, that will produce continual changing reporting Measures to both management and the board. The need for some standard repeated information will not be effected, however this will only account for on average one third to half of the report. The balance of the report will be on the other changing factors that may be positively or negatively disruptive, but will not be required on a continual basis.

The opportunity to alert the organisation to meaningful data is a privilege the CFO has through way of reporting. To monitor, measure and create new measures of meaningful data, is paramount to the organisation's performance and growth.

RESEARCH of the CFO

For many aspiring to transition into a leading CFO role or furthering their skill set in the CFO role, the research available on the CFO position is minimalist and yet the definition of CFO and the roles performed by a CFO are under-represented in publications that present a conflicting definition of the fundamentals of the role. This confliction explains the decision by some countries to adapt the term CPO, Chief Performance Officer, to provide clarity and emphasis on replacing the word Finance. It was this differentiation that sparked my intrigue and subsequent investigation to research why there was such confusion and why the importance of a CFO was being overlooked or not as well recognised by a few major accounting associations and incorrectly defined by organisations promoting paid seminars and memberships for CFO's as finance leaders providing accounting services of a Finance Manager, not a CFO.

The highly respected well-known published business authors such as Steve Bragg, David Parmenter, Robert Kaplan and Jeremy Hope have discussed and a few have published books on the CFO role, yet much further research and clarity was required to reflect today's CFO. The CFO insight came from a highly acclaimed author John Petty, (author of the Australian Business Toolkit with CCH), who was more widely known in Australia and New Zealand for his innovatively designed, created and facilitated strategic workshop to train and upskill CFO's through the CFO of the Future Series for CPA and then CAANZ (formerly ICA). The success of this workshop over fifteen years including many inhouse organisation workshops that were facilitated internationally, awarded the title and recognition to John Petty as the Founder of the CFO training and development. The CFO workshop proved to become the most successful workshop held by both major Australian and New Zealand Accounting Associations. John Petty persuaded the nomenclature of the accounting associations and bodies from a public practice focus to appreciate the importance of industry driven accounting careers. The CFO Workshop provided many tools and techniques such as Rolling Quarterly Forecast, One Day Reporting, Measures that Matter, Customer Profitability Analysis and Strategic Scorecards, of which a few have formed the principle guidance notes for Chartered Accountants and Certified Practicising Accounts.

Dialogue with many CFO's, Practising Tax Agents and Commercial Accountants over the past fifteen years proved what practising CFO's already knew, that the lack of information was a contributing factor of misunderstanding the role of a CFO, that further contributed to the failure to appreciate the role by fellow accountants performing quantitative accounting reports. The general understanding from those in industry, was that a CFO was a senior accountant whose role is to produce a standard set of financial accounts in numeric and comparative format. The thought was an anachronous practice stipulating a CFO would produce historical quantitative reporting rather than qualitative and quantitative forward reporting.

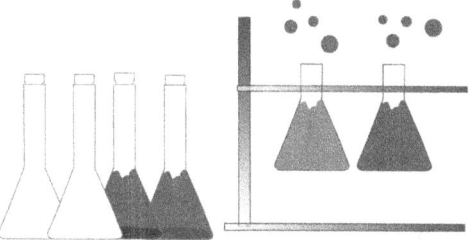

Tools used by a CFO that differ vastly from a Finance Manager and the many tasks required are too abundant and outside the scope of this paper. A future publication to include the tools of a CFO will be released in due course. I recently, accepted the opportunity to facilitate and mentor CFO's as an understudy to John Petty and since his retirement, I am the key facilitator of CFO mentoring and training. This personal insight and continual development of the CFO tools required and its evolving role, provided me a unique opportunity to share with all, the value that a CFO adds to an organisation.

The Future CFO

Technology will continue to impact the way we do business including the depth and scope of how much information we can extract and the capacity to react to change in an effective real time response. It is this ability to engage aptitude instantaneously, and advise of the effect innovation has on the organisation, that pushes the boundary for a CFO to become strategically preeminent within their own frameworks. A requisite to recognise the key drivers both currently and during newly introduced disruptive technology, loads increased pressure on the CFO to be the enabler and driver of strategic roadmaps.

The 2016 IBM publication of the CFO Study has confirmed our research, that the CFO must be able to respond quickly to innovation, be they threats, opportunities or imposing threats having the capability to transition to opportunities where feasible. This is relative to the inhouse technology that is crucial for a CFO and their team. Securing the correct talent that is trained fully in the capability of softwares to trace, record and report tangible data is a pre-requisite. However this is merely the historical data, for once data is available, it is historical and subsequent to alter the result, nonetheless findings can be used to learn for the future.

Increasingly the CFO will focus on the intangible possibilities and effects, to provide the best strategic growth information for the Board and CEO to align with the Organisation's Strategic Goal. Hence the CFO Reporting Framework provides more qualitative data than quantitative. To perceive the risk new technology may impose on the business, requires the CFO to ask the intangible questions of their team, and to promote senior staff to join lobby and advisory groups to remain appraised and proactive. Business once strode by, at a steady slow growth pace, quite often in line with GDP, and without considerable impact from international markets. This antiquated low performance perception offering repeated outcomes is void.

The ability of a CFO to become innovative, being quick to adapt, suggest and create opportunities in a dynamically rapid pace market of technological advancements that effect directly or indirectly on trade, on regulations, on consumer demand, creates the Co-Pilot role to the CEO, the Pilot, being forward thinking and visionary.

Conclusion

In conclusion to our research, we identify the title CFO should be referred to by the letters to mark the Chief Financial Officer title as superseded. The international market shall determine the success of the adaption from CFO to the bespoke CPO title abbreviated for Chief Performance Officer, however the conflict of the current and main alternative use of CPO as the Chief Procurement Officer indicates an overplay of the C-Suite CxO analogies. Debate is welcome as to the limitation consigned to the level, qualifications, experience and heirarchy of executive titles drawing a C-status.

We can say with much evidentiary proof, that the CFO is the second in charge, the co-pilot or co-partner of the CEO and a furtherance to this, should be provided the perogative to ask of the board directly what information they require to assist both organs of board and corporate levels with differential meaningful and measurable reporting that matters.

The type of work performed by the CFO in detail requires a vast array of tools. The matter of tools is extensive and thus outside of the scope of this paper. Due to the level and nature of reporting by a CFO, the educational qualifications of a CFO suggest a minimum post-graduate degree and membership with an international professionally recognised accounting association and a minimum work experience at continuous advancing promotional levels with organisations of fifteen years.

Acknowledgements

Acknowledgement to Mr John Petty for his foundation and promotion of the CFO and many years of research and development of the CFO

Acknowledgement to Sandra Calvert for her years of research, experience and continued advancement through educational training of CFO's.

Reference List

[1] Hatfield, H.R, Sanders, T.H & Burton, N.L 1940, 'Accounting-Principles and Practices: an introductory course', Ginn and company, Boston.

[2] 'What's Behind the Rise of the Chief Performance officer?' 30 August 2016, InsideHR, Accessed 14 January 2018 <http://www.insidehr.com.au/whats-behind-the-rise-of-the-chief-performance-officer/>.

[3] IBM Institute for Business Value 2015, Redefining Boundaries: The Global C-suite Study, Accessed 14 January 2018 <http://www-935.ibm.com/services/c-suite/study/>

[4] IBM Institute for Business Value 2016, Redefining Performance: Insights from the Global C-Suite Study - The CFO Perspective, Accessed 14 January 2018 <http://www-935.ibm.com/services/c-suite/study/studies/cfo-study/>

K. Langfield-Smith, 2008, Strategic management accounting: how far have we come in 25 years?, vol.21, ch2, pp.204-228, (Accessed November 14 2017)

Nelson, E.G, O 1949, 'Science and Accounting', Journal of The Accounting Review, Vol.24, No.4, pp. 354-359, Accessed abstract November 14 2017 <http://www.jstor.org/stable/239799>

Figures

2 IBM Institute for Business Value 2013, 'Boardroom Ties', The Customer-activated Enterprise: Insights from the Global C-suite Study, p.4 Accessed 14 January 2018 <http://www-935.ibm.com/services/c-suite/study/>

www.ingramcontent.com/pod-product-compliance
Lightning Source LLC
Chambersburg PA
CBHW072010030526
44107CB00092B/2579